Taking the Word to Heart

Five Practical Ways to Get a Grip on God's Word

Nancy Taylor

CROSS BOOKS

CrossBooks™
1663 Liberty Drive Suite 300
Bloomington, IN 47403
www.crossbooks.com
Phone: 1-866-879-0502

First published by CrossBooks on.5/22/2009

ISBN: 978-1-6150-7017-6 (sc)

Printed in the United States of America
Bloomington, Indiana
This book is printed on acid-free paper

Taking The Word To Heart is a joy to read and a treasure to hide deep in one's life. The book is intensely practical and easy to use. I found it's combination of spiritual tools and personal illustrations well balanced. Pass it on!

Waylon B. Moore
Founder and President of Missions Unlimited

Without a doubt, scripture memory is the heartbeat of Nancy Taylor. It is God's Word that sustains, motivates and captivates us. Nancy does a tremendous job giving the "nuts and bolts" along with the inspiration to place God's Word in our hearts. You can trust this book to challenge and lead you closer to the Lord.

Gregg Matte
Pastor, Houston's First Baptist Church

"*Taking The Word To Heart* is a passionate appeal for all believers to deeply embrace and treasure God's eternal Word. The cry of the author to memorize, meditate upon and be transformed by God's Word flows out of an authentic lifestyle. I was moved by how the author does not speak from theory, but from a life that has become permeated by God's wisdom. The book provides very practical advice for making God's Word a part of everyday life and ministry. Recent research shows that most Christians do not memorize and meditate upon the Bible. The Body of Christ can be greatly strengthened by embracing the challenge of *Taking The Word To Heart.*"

Brad J. Waggoner
BH Publishing Group

Acknowledgments

I want to thank . . .

My Lord Jesus Christ for His powerful Word that continues to transform my life.

My husband and best friend, William, for his constant encouragement.

My children, Will and Sarah for living out the truth of 3 John 4: "I have no greater joy than to hear that my children are walking in the truth."

Pat Lewis for her early editing and for cheering me on to the finish line.

My accountability partners, Vicky Wright, Diane Bagby, Denise Munton, Carolyn O'Neal, and Sue Hurst for their support and prayers.

Josh Alexander for his design work on the cover.

Brad Waggoner for introducing me to Cross Books and their wonderful staff.

Table of Contents

Introduction

At Home in My Heart

God's Word is at long last at home in my heart. I can now say that hiding God's Word in my heart has enabled me to take ownership of God's Word, which has provided many opportunities to minister to those who are weary or brokenhearted, and most importantly, allowed me to experience a deeper, more intimate relationship with Christ. After coming to Christ as a child, I remained immature in my faith until I discovered the habit that would transform my life. I accepted Christ out of a desire to be secure and safe. I needed the security and peace that God offered and that I lacked as a child of an alcoholic father. My dad was a wonderful, fun-loving man when sober, but became verbally abusive when he was drunk. The years of storing up these defeating words in my mind wreaked havoc on me emotionally, mentally, and spiritually. In my last year of college, I discovered a whole new world that I had never known before. I met Christians who actually lived out their faith and enjoyed it! I saw something in these people that I wanted desperately in my life. They knew God in such a real way that I had never experienced. They prayed, read their Bibles, and talked about God working in their lives. Through these new friends, I discovered what it meant to *grow* as a Christian. I was introduced to new disciplines such as daily devotions, Bible study, prayer journaling, and scripture memorization. The disciplines were just what I needed, or so it seemed, to gain that security and structure that had eluded me as a child. The roller coaster ride began. I would keep up with these disciplines for a while, and then a crisis or an *event* would come along in my life that would interrupt my discipline. I was in the trap of "all or nothing" thinking. I believed a lie that said, "Nancy, if you can't perform perfectly, then just give up!" God guided me out of this trap by showing me how to grip tightly the Word of God, and in turn he totally transformed my life. This book is a result of my passion for hiding God's Word in my heart and a desire for sharing this passion with others.

Getting to Know God and His Word

My journey from defeat to delight began when the Lord showed me that the only weapon I had in my quest to live a victorious life was the *memorized* Word of God. I was in a Bible study that dealt with tearing down strongholds. The biggest stronghold in my life was my thought life. My mind had continued to cycle back into negative and destructive thoughts that kept me from experiencing the life God had planned for me. Once aware of my stronghold, I made an unwavering commitment to store up the weapon of the Word so that I would have an ample supply of ammunition against the enemy of my thought life! I made a commitment to memorize one verse a week for fifty-two weeks, with the goal of quoting all fifty-two verses at the conclusion of that year. Never could I have conceived what God had in store for me through this simple commitment to hide his Word in my heart. My knowledge of God increased, and along with this knowledge, my heart was filled with the love for God that Deuteronomy 6:5 speaks of: "Love the Lord your God with all your heart and with all your soul and with all your strength." What began as a commitment to do something for myself became all about what God wanted to do in me through his hidden Word.

He not only transformed my way of thinking, but also taught me how to delight in his truth when faced with daily inconveniences and even when life brought overwhelming circumstances. I learned the truth of Luke 6:45, "… for His mouth speaks from that which fills his heart." In the English dictionary you will find that delight means "to give great joy or pleasure to; to be highly pleased, rejoice." However, in Hebrew, the language of the Old Testament, there are several words that are translated as delight which have richer meaning. One such word, *chapets*, is found in Psalm 1:2, "His delight is in the law of the Lord," and means "a valuable thing." One who places great value in God's Word experiences delight. The word *chapets* is later found in scripture in Psalm 40:8 (NASB), "I delight to do Your will, O my God; Your law is within my heart," and refers to one being inclined to do something or bending to it. In Psalm 37:4, the familiar exhortation to "delight yourself in the Lord" is translated from the Hebrew word *anag*, meaning "to be soft or pliable." When we tie these meanings and verses together, we come to the conclusion that when one delights themselves in the Lord and in his Word, they are valuing God's Word in such a way that they are inclined to have a pliable heart and mind to the things of God.

We trust in what we delight in, and if we delight in whining and complaining, then that is what comes out of our mouths the minute we find ourselves in a difficult situation. I am learning to delight in his Word and have been amazed at the truth that flows from my mouth whenever I find myself in a stressful or overwhelming circumstance. Jesus instructs us to listen to what he says and not to our natural inclinations in Matthew 5:44, "But I say to you, love your enemies and pray for those who persecute you." That is not natural, but spiritual. It means having a soft heart and opened mind to listen to God's Word above your own thoughts. My mind was more attuned and my heart more moldable to the voice of Christ rather than my own, self-focused thoughts when I consistently kept the commitment to weekly delight in God's Word.

Getting a Grip

Despair and depression do not come along as often, and when they try to invade my life, I have learned to use the weapon of God's Word to fight against those thoughts. He has revealed to me that if I am depressed, it is because I am impressed with my own circumstances and not impressed with him and his powerful truth. God continues to show me that I must not rationalize my lies, but realize his truth when confronted with temptations, character flaws, and challenging events in my life. It is as if God is holding out his Word and saying to me, "Get a grip on my truth!" When I am obedient to dwell on the truth hidden in my heart, I find that his truth, in turn, gets a grip on my thoughts, emotions, and behavior.

Memorize

Memorize the Word with Purpose

Just as it takes five fingers to have a good grip on what is being held in one's hand, it also takes five essential parts to provide a solid grip on the truth of God's Word. As I began my fifty-two-week journey to memorize scripture, I discovered that memorization was just the beginning step and would only provide minimal strength to my grip. It was as if I was trying to hold a large suitcase using only my pinky! However, the pinky finger is an essential part for a solid grip; so is the act of memorizing the verses merely the first step to the complete process of gripping God's Word.

Purpose

Through memorizing scripture, we will gain a greater knowledge of who this God is that we are instructed to love with all our heart, soul, and strength (Deut. 6:5). What better place to go than God's Word to find out just who this God is we are instructed to love! Knowledge of God is not only one of the purposes for memorizing scripture, but it is a life-changing benefit as well. Second Peter 1:3 tells us that God has given us everything we need for life and godliness through our knowledge of him. Not only will God's Word help us become better acquainted with our mighty God but also as our counselor, he will provide us with everything we need in life through the God-breathed Word. Jesus Christ was the Word wrapped in flesh (John 1:14). The hope that we as Christians all share is in the mystery that Christ lives in us (Col. 1:27). Second Timothy 3:16–17 tells us that God's Word was given to us by him and that it is useful for all of life: teaching, rebuking, correcting, and training in righteousness.

Memorizing scripture can become a legalistic action if done with the wrong motive. Chuck Swindoll has defined *legalism* as "conformity to a standard for the purpose of exalting self. The purpose of our discipline should be to order our lives in such a way that we are available to be used by God."[1] In fact, Jesus warns us to "beware of practicing our righteousness before men to be noticed by them" (Matt. 6:1). Treasuring the Word in our hearts should be done with godly intention and purpose. Other purposes for taking God's Word to heart include overcoming temptation, renewing and preparing the mind, receiving direction and guidance, developing godly character, and establishing an effective prayer life.

Overcoming Temptation

The New American Standard Bible translation states, in Psalm 119:11, that we are to "treasure" God's Word in our hearts, so that we will not sin against God. The New International Version states that the Word is "hidden" in our hearts. I have a problem with using the word *hidden*, as I have hidden many a Christmas present in July but have totally forgotten about it until sometime in January. Whereas, the word *treasure* reminds me of the strand of pearls given to me by my husband in honor of our fifteenth wedding anniversary. Because I treasure those pearls, I keep them in a special velvet pouch tucked inside a

1 Cynthia Heald, *Becoming a Woman of Excellence* (Colorado Springs: NavPress, 2005), p. 77.

wooden box for safekeeping. I keep them there so that I will know exactly where they are when I want to wear them. So it is with the Word of God. When I am tempted to sin, the treasured Word of God is tucked in my heart, so that I will know where it is when I need it! I can still be overcome by temptation unless I cry out to God, seeking and asking him to activate his Word in my life. When we cry out to him, he will accomplish what concerns us (Ps. 57:2). God is so powerful and sovereign that he could just put in our minds and mouths a scripture that we had never memorized in our attempt to resist the enemy. However, I have never had that happen! It was only after I began to memorize scripture, asking God to use it in my life, that he would bring it to my mind and empower me to submit to his truth and resist the enemy. While exiting the freeway in pursuit of a forbidden dessert at one of my favorite restaurants, the treasured Word came roaring into my thoughts before I could act on the temptation. The truth of 1 Corinthians 10:13 pounded in my head: "No temptation has seized you except what is common to man. And God is faithful; he will not let you be tempted beyond what you can bear. But when you are tempted, he will also provide a way out so that you can stand up under it." I cried out at that moment, "Lord, show me the way out!" As I drove onto the exit ramp, I stayed in the left-hand lane, taking a left turn that led straight to the safety of my home! The treasured Word was just where I put it for such a time as this.

Renewing and Preparing the Mind

Peter exhorts believers to "prepare your minds for action, be self controlled, set your hope fully on the grace to be given you when Jesus Christ is revealed." A couple of years ago, I ran my first and only half-marathon. I didn't show up on the day of the race without first preparing for six months. My goal was to first finish the race and then to do so in a somewhat respectable time frame. As I began my preparation, my intention was to walk the entire 13.1 miles, but as I day by day followed my plan, I became stronger and would jog a mile here and there along the way. In the month before the race, it became evident to me that I could possibly run at least half of the 13.1 miles. On the day of the race, I paired up with a young friend of mine, who began to run, and so I eagerly followed suit. As we ran, the cheering supporters along the course encouraged us so much that I ended up only walking a few miles of the race and finished the race in a much better time frame than I had expected! Preparing my body and mind for the race gave me the strength to not only compete, but to finish.

Garbage in, garbage out is a popular computer phrase, yet it clearly communicates how the human brain also functions. Prior to my scripture memory journey, my mind had become so filled with negative thoughts that I began to believe the lies and my behavior mimicked my thought life. I had a constant tape playing in my head that made such statements as, "I will never be good enough," or "God would never forgive me for that," and even "I am too old to change now!" Romans 12:2 commands us, "Do not conform any longer to the pattern of this world, but be transformed by the renewing of your mind. Then you will be able to test and approve what God's will is—his good, pleasing, and perfect will." The battle is won or lost in the mind! Second Corinthians 10:5 explains clearly our battle plans: "We demolish arguments and every pretension that sets itself up against the knowledge of God, and *we take captive every thought* to make it obedient to Christ." My dog loves to take *me* for a walk! He drags me along on his leash for as long as he can get away with it. Eventually I tug on the leash and command him to heel or sit! In the same way, we must renew our undisciplined thinking by taking the leash of every thought and intentionally commanding the thought to line up with the truth of God's Word. We must be prepared with the proper leash if we want to captivate our thoughts with scripture. The only way we will be able to renew the mind through taking our thoughts captive is to have stored up the Word in our hearts.

The Word that is lodged in our hearts prepares us for the life-path we are given. When we use the Spirit-given self-control needed to prepare day by day, our eyes will be fully fixed on the hands of Christ offering his encouraging gifts of grace. It is his grace that allows us to finish the race set before us. However, in order to run your race as a winner, the mind must be renewed and prepared.

Gaining Direction and Guidance

Seeking to gain discipline in my eating habits, I memorized Titus 2:11–12, "For the grace of God that brings salvation has appeared to all men. It teaches us to say 'No' to ungodliness and worldly passions and to live self-controlled, upright and godly lives in this present age." The NASB put it another way: "to live sensibly, righteously and godly." I was determined to learn how to say no to overeating, but the Lord had another use for His truth. After losing a good amount of weight, I rediscovered the joy of shopping. I was preparing for some upcoming speaking and teaching opportunities and realized that I needed some new clothes to fit my newly discovered shape. As I was shopping one day, it seemed that everything I brought into the fitting room fit perfectly and looked great on me. To borrow a sport term, "I was in the zone!" Since everything was on sale, I rationalized that I could buy it all and so I did! It wasn't until I was standing in my closet looking at all I had bought that the Holy Spirit brought to mind Titus' words. Then I sought God's guidance, which I admit I was a little late in seeking, by asking Him if my purchase was sensible, righteous, and godly. Using God's Word as my counsel, I determined I should take half of my purchases back that day. As I did, a huge burden of guilt was lifted off of my shoulders, as I knew God had directed my steps so clearly through His hidden Word.

God created you with purpose and for a purpose. His purpose was to love and be loved. Recently I heard someone say that we are God's dream come true! Psalm 139 tells us that our Creator wrote down all the days we were to live before we ever breathed our first breath! He knit us together while still in our mother's womb. He knows the days we live and will live and what those days will bring. Therefore, since we know that he has given us everything we need for life through our knowledge of him, and that our knowledge of him comes straight from his Word, then his Word will show us which way to go and how to go that way! A verse I pray back to God often is Psalm 143:8, "Let the morning bring me word of your unfailing love, for I have put my trust in you. Show me the way I should go, for to you I lift up my soul." He counsels us with his love and gives us direction as we trust him and grip tightly his instructive, loving, and living Word.

Developing Godly Character

I often will read a Psalm a day and a Proverb a day for my devotional time. The Proverb generally brings me conviction and the Psalm brings me compassion. It reminds me of God's amazing power to convict through the Holy Spirit, and in the same moment, bring his compassionate Word to soften the blow. One morning I read Proverbs 14:23, "In all labor there is profit, but mere talk leads only to poverty." Those divine words pierced my heart and showed me that I was not living a life of integrity at work. I was leading people to commit to discipline their lives mentally, emotionally, physically, and spiritually, but I was failing to do the very things I was teaching. I was just talking the talk and not walking it. That morning I shared this scripture with those I worked with and confessed my character poverty. It was just a short time later that I began to memorize God's Word with passion and with the motivation of this very verse, not wanting to be just a talker but a laborer. The Lord continues to use this hidden word in my life to remind me often to work and live with integrity.

Peter acknowledges that God gives us "his very great and precious promises . . . so that through them *we* may participate in the divine nature and escape the corruption in the world caused by evil desires" (2 Peter 1:4). God's Word equips us for a new way of living. God recreates us once we receive the gift of salvation and we are made new in his eyes. We take on the righteousness of God first by simply responding to his call of redemption. Then once we have responded, we become new creatures—baby believers. We must crave his Word—pure milk—so that we can grow up and mature. Paul informs the

Colossians that Epaphras wrestled in prayer for them so that they would stand firm in all the will of God, mature and fully assured. In my own life, maturity has come only when I have sought to move through obedience to God's Word. It is not easy, but it will produce a harvest of right living to those who have been trained by it. We discipline ourselves, not for discipline's sake, but for the joy set before us—the harvest. (See Romans 12:11; Hebrews 12:2.)

Cultivating an Effective Prayer Life

While memorizing John 15:7, I had an "aha" moment in which I discovered another purpose for hiding God's Word in my heart. As I meditated on the words "If you abide in me and my Words abide in you, ask whatever you wish and it shall be done for you," it became clear to me that praying the truths and promises of God's Word would result in praying God's will. I began to attach people and their prayer needs to memorized verses, which helped me to remember the reference; and it kept my prayers focused and in line with God's will. At fifteen years old, my son was drawing more and more into himself and was very depressed. I felt that the only way he would come out of his darkness was to grasp just how much God loved him. I cried out to the Lord and he showed me a scripture to pray for him. I quickly memorized the verse by praying it daily and also asking all the prayer warriors I knew to pray Ephesians 3:16–19 for him: "That *God* would grant my son, according to his glorious riches, to be strengthened with power through his Spirit in the inner man … being rooted and grounded in love … able to comprehend … the breadth, and length, and height, and depth of God's love." NASB Through praying the powerful, life-changing truth of God's Word, my faith was strengthened, my prayer life refocused, and within a few weeks, my son's life took a dramatic turn. He came out of the his depressed state and the joy of the Lord became so evident that before the year was out, he was leading worship at his high school's weekly chapel services.

Memorize

Manned with a Plan

Just having the "want to" of scripture memory will not accomplish the goal of hiding God's Word in your heart for a lifetime. As someone once said, "If you shoot for nothing, that is exactly what you get!" If you want to memorize scripture, then establish a plan and work it out until it works for you. It's just like shopping for a pair of shoes—sometimes it takes trying on a couple of plans before you find one that fits your learning style and personality. I will share a plan with you that worked for me. Try it on and then keep what works for you and adapt the rest to fit your learning lifestyle. Also, when a pair of shoes wears out and no longer fits comfortably, you either take them to the repair shop to have them refurbished, or you throw them out and buy a new pair. Therefore, if on your journey of memorizing scripture you find yourself in a rut, then change it up, refurbish your plan, or take on a totally new one. The idea is to stay on the journey and not allow the plan to hinder you from progress. Work it out.

What Verses Should You Memorize?

I was in my Sunday morning Bible study when the teacher mentioned Micah 7:7–8, just as a side note to the main lesson. I had been in a battle with a specific sin issue in my life and had experienced defeat when the words "Do not gloat over me, my enemy! Though I have fallen, I will rise. Though I sit in darkness, the LORD will be my light," came rushing into my ears, straight to my heart. I began memorizing the verse that very day and have been quoting it ever since whenever faced with discouragement in the midst of momentary defeat. I would suggest that you choose a scripture verse to memorize that has special meaning and purpose for your life. For example, if you are struggling with a specific sin in your life and desire to have victory over that sin, then 1 Corinthians 10:13 would be a great place to start. When I am struggling with that old sin of overeating, this verse reminds me that there is a way out of the tempting situation. "No temptation has seized you except what is common to man. And God is faithful; he will not let you be tempted beyond what you can bear. But when you are tempted, he will also provide a way out so that you can stand up under it." Memorizing scriptures that deal with specific topics such as God's character, relationships, marriage, God's will, peace, encouragement, and love may all be practical and relevant for your life. Choosing scriptures that meet specific needs in your life or the lives of those you are praying for will be verses that will be easier to memorize and will take root much quicker.

Keep a list of verses that you would like to memorize in your prayer journal, computer, or personal organizer/calendar. You will find that God pricks your heart and mind with scripture while in Bible study classes, listening to speakers or sermons, and while reading daily devotionals. When a verse speaks to you in a very specific and powerful way, then put it on the list of verses to memorize. Memorize verses that not only have special meaning and purpose, but also those that are immediately relevant to your life.

To keep from setting yourself up for failure, it is best to stick with one to two verses a week. Once you become consistent and confident in your memorization, you may want to begin working on passages, chapters, or even entire books of scripture. I would never encourage someone to begin memorizing whole chapters before they got a handle on the verse-a-week system. Remember that it is not the quantity of verses you memorize, but the quality of life application you gain from each verse memorized.

What Translation Should I Use?

I began memorizing verses from the New American Standard Bible since it was the Bible I had used since I was in college. It was easy to memorize due to its poetic language. However, I noticed that sharing these verses with un-churched friends and acquaintances seemed awkward because its use of Old English. I eventually began to study and read mostly from the New International Version and found that it was more conversational—and thus more user-friendly—when sharing with nonbelievers. I would caution against memorizing large amounts of scripture from paraphrases, as they tend to be very wordy and are not always as biblically accurate as the translations. The key is to memorize from the version that you are most comfortable with and one that you use most often.

Working the Plan

Positive Attitude

Once you have a verse to memorize that is purposeful and practical in the version that you use regularly, then let the memorizing begin. Start with a positive attitude and a willingness to be intentional in your pursuit. Proverbs 14:23, one of the first scriptures I memorized, addresses the need to be intentional: "All hard work brings a profit, but mere talk leads only to poverty." I reached a point where I was tired of just talking about my desire to memorize scripture and wanted to walk that desire out. When you string together several days of intentionally hiding God's word in your heart, it begins to develop into a habit. I have found in my own life that I become what I habitually do. If I make a habit out of overeating, I become an overeater. If I make a habit of complaining, I become a complainer. Conversely, if I habitually thank God for each day's blessings, I become grateful, and if I make a habit of memorizing scripture and walking it out in my life, I become a woman of the Word. Once you intentionally make scripture memory a habit in your life, then you will become what Psalm 1 speaks of as "a tree firmly planted by streams of water, which yields it fruit in season, whose leaf does not wither and in whatever he does prospers."

My fifty-two verses in fifty-two weeks plan began with spiral index cards. The spirals usually contain fifty 3x5" index cards. Since there are fifty-two weeks in a year, you will be able to carry this spiral with you for an entire year, enabling you to be constantly reminded of the verses you have memorized, as well as the one you are working on presently. On each card, I wrote the scripture reference and the date on the top line. Knowing the reference is very important whenever the Lord gives you opportunity to share the verse with someone. Giving them the reference empowers them to go and look up the truth for themselves. Dating each card will give a timeline to when you memorized the verse and will help you associate the activity or season in your life with the verses you memorized. Then the scripture would be written on the following lines, with the reference written once again at the bottom of the card. On the back of the card, only the reference would be written. This will be helpful when reviewing the verses.

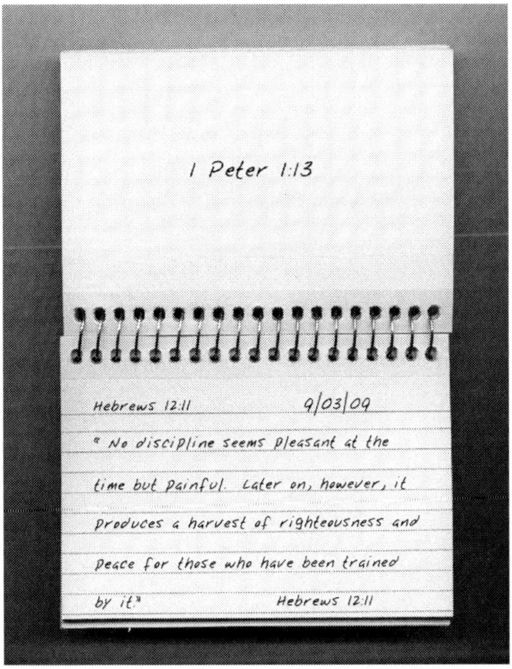

Determine Your Learning Style

I do my best thinking when I take my morning walks or when I am cleaning my house. Memorizing scripture while I am moving helps me to focus better on the words and their meaning. Recognizing how I learn best has helped me to continue on this scripture memory journey.

If you are an auditory learner, then singing the scripture memory verses, reading them aloud, or recording them will be very helpful in the memorization process. If you are a visual learner, then writing the verses out and repeatedly reading through them will cement them into your mind visually. If you are a tactile kinesthetic learner, or you learn by doing, then creating motions for the words or using sign language will enable you to more easily recall the verse.

Attach Daily Tasks to Scripture Memory

When my daughter was in high school she did not have a car, so I spent a good deal of time in the car with her as I carted her around to various activities. While in the car, I would have her quiz me on my verses. It was a great accountability tool and provided some teachable moments with my daughter. The bottom line is to make scripture memorization as much a part of your life as brushing your teeth or eating breakfast and as enjoyable as eating chocolate cake!

When your words came, I ate them; they were my joy and my heart's delight, for I bear your name, O LORD God Almighty. Jeremiah 15:16

After determining your learning style, then attach your scripture memorization to a daily task, such as driving to work, walking on the treadmill, or eating lunch. Use these daily tasks as opportunities to memorize and review your verses. Even meal times can be used as a time to share your verse with those at your table. Close email communications by typing in your weekly memory verse or make a point to say your memory verse every time you brush your teeth.

Passage

I had read and heard many times 1 Peter 5:7: "[Cast] all your anxiety on Him because He cares for you." This verse contains a wonderful truth that God cares for us and that we can trust him to care for the things that bring us anxiety. However, when I read the next verse, 1 Peter 5:8, it says, "Be self-controlled and alert, your enemy the devil, prowls around like a roaring lion, looking for someone to devour." By simply looking at what follows casting my cares onto God, I see the urgency of the command. Casting our cares onto the Lord takes self-control and requires our alertness to our need to do so. When we carry our burdens around, we are weighted down and easily devoured by the enemy of depression, anger, and other such emotions that are contrary to what God would have us experience. God cares, but the devil devours. Before starting the actual memory work, read the entire passage that surrounds the verse you have chosen to memorize. This will give more insight and understanding into the verse and will guard against using the verse incorrectly or out of context. Reading the passage usually leads me to other verses that I write on my list of verses to be memorized, because they give me even more insight into God's Word and more ammunition to use against the enemy!

Paste Reference to Verse

For years I habitually said, "Somewhere in the Bible it says …" I knew the truth, but was unable to direct others to it and was unable to prove that what I was saying was in fact really in the Bible. It is crucial to paste the reference to the verse as you memorize. When asked to provide your address to someone, you do not simply give the street, but also provide the street number. So it is with scripture. Knowing the reference gives credibility to the truth. Treat the reference of the verse like the first word of the verse. For example, Romans 15:13 says, "May the God of hope fill you with all joy and peace as you trust in Him, so that you may overflow with hope by the power of the Holy Spirit." When saying this verse over and over, always begin with "Romans 15:13" and do not even pause before saying the first word of the verse. Say it just like you would your address. Saying the reference and the first few words as one phrase will help to attach the reference to those words, thus triggering you to remember the entire verse.

Associate the Reference

When memorizing Romans 15:13, I asked the Lord how could I remember those numbers. I then noticed that the numbers fifteen and thirteen were the exact ages of my children. Then I realized that they were both teenagers. Teenagers are known for *roaming around*, so the reference was associated with *roaming* (Romans) *teenagers,* ages fifteen and thirteen. And since I was the mother of roaming teenagers, ages fifteen and thirteen, I needed the God of hope to fill me with all joy and peace! Thus this phrase, "Romans 15:13: May the God of hope," is cemented in my brain forever! Once again, find a system that works best for you. Look for number patterns within the references, such as even or odd numbers, multiples, or sums. Sometimes it may come down to just repeating it over and over every day for a week before you can remember it. Remember to be intentional and ask God to help you find ways to associate the reference to the verse.

Phrase by Phrase

Colossians 3:12 includes a list of godly attributes. As I meditated on the words in the list, I noticed the first letters of each word were *C, K, H, G,* and *P.* As I looked at *C* and *K,* I thought of my friend Kay, who always lavishes her friends with hugs. *So C and K* would stand for "See Kay." The *H and G* would stand for "hugs," and the *P* would remind me to say "please." So, *C-K-H-G-P* was attached to "See *(C)* Kay *(K)* for hugs *(H, G),* please *(P).*" After spending the time to make this association, I have never forgotten that Colossians 3:12 says, "Therefore as God's chosen people, holy and dearly loved, clothe yourselves with compassion, kindness, humility, gentleness and patience."

Breaking a verse—especially one that is longer—into smaller phrases helps with the memorization process. As you read the phrases over and over, you may notice patterns, rhymes, or lists within the verse. Taking the time to search the memory verse for these patterns compares to building a house on a firm foundation. If you intentionally build a firm foundation of gluing the reference to the verse and breaking the verse into phrases as you search out patterns, rhymes, and lists, the verse will stand strong in your mind, heart, and memory!

Perfectly

Learn each verse word-perfect. Have you ever noticed that when asked to recite the pledge of allegiance or sing a verse of "Amazing Grace," people will recite or sing the same words? No one paraphrases the words, or says, "Well, it says something like …" We all remember nursery rhymes and songs learned in our childhood and can quote from memory the exact words. That is because we remember what we learned perfectly. Practice makes permanent. There is a degree of danger in this statement because we may well practice something incorrectly, and thus our practice becomes a bad habit. Practicing the exact words of scripture will insure that your practice will make perfect, enabling you to recall the words many years later.

Think back to all the nursery rhymes and children's songs that you learned as a young child. If I gathered a few of you together in a room and asked you to sing "Mary Had a Little Lamb," more than likely, you all would sing every word the same. You learned the song perfectly, so you remember it perfectly! We do not want to make scripture memory a legalistic task with no room for grace. However, we do want to hide the complete truth in our hearts, not just partial truth or a watered-down version. Take time to write out your verses correctly, not subtracting or adding any words. As you memorize the verse, and as you review it, take time to check your accuracy, so that you will know *the whole truth and nothing but the truth!*

Partner

When I got serious about memorizing scripture, I told all my friends about my goal to memorize a verse a week. I not only told them what I was doing, I also asked them to join my journey by holding me accountable. I asked friends and co-workers to make a point of asking me to quote the verse I was working on each week. And sometimes to my embarrassment, they followed through! Accountability is an essential ingredient when developing any good or godly habit. Therefore, partner with someone as you seek to make scripture memorization a habit in your life. "As iron sharpens iron, so one man sharpens another" (Prov. 27:17). It is important to ask at least one person who will encourage you in your journey and who you know will be faithful to ask you weekly for your memory verse. One word of caution: It is best not to ask the one holding you accountable to join you in memorizing scripture (assuming they are not already memorizing scripture), as sometimes that person will not hold you accountable when they are struggling with their own memorization, or they could possibly not have the same level of commitment and thus they may become a hindrance rather than a help to your journey. This will also avoid feelings of guilt or embarrassment. It is best to have a coach as an accountability partner and not necessarily a fellow teammate!

Persistent Review

As I write this book, I sit beside a basket full of scripture memory spirals. They are worn, torn, and stained. I have learned that if I keep them with me, the Word stays with me and I review them more often. It has been said that it takes ninety to 100 days of reviewing a verse before it truly becomes your own. I find that using the index card spiral of fifty cards makes this process much easier and more convenient. I will keep two spirals with me throughout any given day—one contains the verses I am learning presently or during the current year, and the other contains verses from another year that I will review that day. The next day my current spiral continues to be my constant companion and I pick up another past year's spiral for a one-day review. Review on a rotating basis, ensuring that you review verses older than one year at least once a week. Taking the verses with you wherever you go will be a constant reminder of your commitment to hide God's Word in your heart. Just like taking along a bottle of water on a long hike reminds you of your body's need for re-hydration, the memory verse spiral is a reminder that … "you do not live on bread alone, but on every Word of God" (Matt. 4:4). Carry the verses with you so you will be ready to review while standing in line at the grocery store, while in the waiting room at the doctor's office, or during your afternoon break time. Intentionally use your *free* moments each day to fill your mind and heart with truth by persistently reviewing your memory verses. John Maxwell says, "Commitment is not an emotion; it is a character quality that enables us to reach our goals."[2] Do not allow your emotions to keep you from your commitment to hide God's Word in your heart.

2 John Maxwell, *Leadership Wired* (InJoy Inc, April 2002, Vol. 5, Issue 7)

Hebrews 12:11

"No discipline seems pleasant at the time but painful. Later on, however, it produces a harvest of righteousness and peace for those who have been trained by it."

Taking it to Heart

Day One: Get Started!

1. Select a verse to memorize based on one of the purposes for scripture memorization: overcoming temptation, renewing and preparing the mind, receiving direction and guidance, developing godly character, and establishing an effective prayer life. (See appendix.) Ask the Lord to reveal to you what area of your life needs the light of his truth.
2. Using an index card spiral, write the reference and date at the top of the first card and then write the verse. Then read the entire chapter that the verse has been taken from to gain more insight.
3. Carry the verse with you wherever you go and review while waiting in line, brushing your teeth, ironing your clothes, or walking on the treadmill.
4. Connect the reference to the first few words. Locate patterns, phrases, or key words. Apply to circumstance you are now in. Pray the verse.

Days Two–Six: Live Intentionally!

1. Repeat the process you completed on steps three and four of day one.
2. Pray and ask God for an accountability partner.

3. Seek out a partner who will faithfully hold you accountable.

Day Seven: Review Day!

1. Try to write out the passage in your prayer journal without looking at your index spiral. Check to see how you did. Make note of any special insights you discovered or ways you have practically applied the passage to your life.
2. Review the verses throughout the day, striving for word-perfect memorization.

Meditate

Chew on the Word and Ponder its Meaning

Meditation has helped me to value *every* word of scripture. Taking time to focus on each word and asking the Lord questions about its purpose opens my eyes to a more personalized message of the Word. While meditating on Psalm 18:28–30, I read it over and over again while emphasizing a different word each time and the words "*my* darkness" pierced my heart. I suddenly realized afresh that darkness is not just out in the open, but it can be hidden within me. I have darkness, but God shines his light of truth on those dark thoughts, empowering me to leap over walls of discouragement and concern. This helped me to gain further understanding—not only of the scripture, but also of who God is and how he relates personally to me. I had been caught up in allowing the dark memories of my past to keep me from pressing forward in the future God had for me, but once this Word gripped my heart, freedom from the darkness came rushing in to give me renewed hope and vision.

If you have ever been in a play, choir program, or dance recital, you have experienced a dress rehearsal. A dress rehearsal is a final rehearsal, in full costume and with lights, music, and effects, before the production is given its first public performance. Meditating on scripture is a dress rehearsal of real life. When mediating on scripture, you are going over and over in your mind the words and meaning of the scripture.

One Hebrew word for meditation means to muse, or rehearse in one's mind.[3]

The meditation process is especially helpful in memorizing scripture and applying it to real-life situations. As you meditate on scripture, you are practicing how you would live out the truth of what you are memorizing. It is "setting your mind on heavenly things" (Col. 3:1–2). Memorizing scripture is just the "pinky finger" part of getting a grip on God's Word. The next part of the grip is when the ring finger is added. It is generally where we wear our wedding ring or class ring, which symbolizes commitment and accomplishment. Meditating on God's Word takes a commitment of time, but yields the accomplishment of a deeper knowledge of scripture. It is easy to become lazy in our walk with Christ and depend on others to constantly feed us spiritually. Meditation is a tool that will equip you to nourish yourself with the life-giving bread of God's Word.

Waylon Moore introduced me to meditation in his book, *Living God's Word.*[4] He has given me permission to share the meditation process with you.

First Step: Perimeter of the Verse

I was memorizing the last verse of John 16: "I have told you these things so that in me you may have peace. In this world you will have trouble. But take heart! I have overcome the world," and began to question what "these things" were Jesus spoke of that would bring peace. Taking the time to read the prior verses, I discovered that he told the disciples he would

3 Wikipedia , the free encyclopedia
4 Waylon B. Moore, *Living God's Word* (Nashville: LifeWay Press, 1997) p.50.

send the Holy Spirit to guide them into all truth, reminding them of Jesus' words and of his love for them. Because of these things, we will experience the peace he speaks of in verse 33.

To begin the meditation process, relate the verse to be memorized with the verses surrounding it. In other words, we must be careful to not take a verse out of context, thus losing the intended meaning. Reading the full chapter surrounding the verse being memorized sheds light, gives insight, and helps broaden the scope of the verse. This is the same step used in memorizing, which was mentioned earlier. When reading the passage, be alert to observations and questions that may come to your mind. It is what my college English professor called "intentional reading."

Second Step: Paraphrase the Verse

A friend of mine always paraphrases her verses by putting her name in the verse or changing the word "men" to "women." As she paraphrases the verse, she makes it personal. A verse we memorized together was Proverbs 10:19: "When there are many words, transgression is unavoidable, but he who restrains his lips is wise." (NASB) I was memorizing it to help with my weakness of talking when I should be quiet. My friend, however, attached it to her struggle with overeating and paraphrased it like this, "When there is much food around, overeating is unavoidable, but he who restrains his lips [literally!] is wise." The Word spoke to both of us in different ways to meet specific issues in our lives. Writing the verse in your own words helps to cement the verse's meaning in your mind. Paraphrasing the verse makes it "yours" and gives you ownership of the Word.

Thus, paraphrasing the verse will bring about more personal application.

Third Step: Pulverize the Verse

The meditation process has been compared to the process by which a cow chews on her cud. It is chewing on the Word over and over again. Pulverizing a verse allows you to spotlight each word contained in the verse. Repeatedly read the verse, each time emphasizing a different word, until you have highlighted each word. By the time you have read the verse that many times, you generally have it memorized! As you read over the verse, one word may seem to leap off the page or "stand out" more than the others. Begin to ask yourself questions beginning with the words *who, why, where, what, when,* and *how* regarding the "standout" word. This is a great way to study the Bible without any extra resources. It also will enable you to recall the verse more readily as you will have spent time with the verse and will have a personalized insight linked to the verse.

Fourth Step: Personalize the Verse

James 1:22 reminds me often to do what the Word says; not to just read or even memorize it, but to actually do it! After you have a better understanding of the perimeter and have pulverized the verse, the Holy Spirit will begin to convict you of a sin or convince you of a truth that you need personally for a specific challenge or circumstance. When this happens, apply the balm of the Word to a specific hurt, need, or challenge. This is where sanctification takes place—where we begin to deny ourselves, taking up our crosses and obediently following the Lord's Word and way.

Fifth Step: Pray the Verse

Praying the verse for yourself and others helps you to glue the truth of the memorized Word to specific needs in your life or others. Ask God to use the verse in your life each time you review the verse and use it as a prayer reminder to pray for the needs of others as well.

You may want to repeat this process for a few days or even the entire week in which you are memorizing the verse. I have not only used this process in my quiet times with the Lord, but also have used it as I waited in a doctor's office, drove in the car, and as I exercised. You may copy the next page and place it with your scripture memory cards or in your prayer journal as a meditation guide.

The Meditation Process

Scripture reference: ______________________________

Step One: Understand the perimeter of the verse:

Step Two: Paraphrase the verse:

____

____

Step Three: Pulverize the verse:

Emphasize a different word in separate readings. Choose one word that is key to the message of the verse for you.

Ask questions about the word and answer them if you can:

Who? ______________________________________

What? _____________________________________

When? _____________________________________

Where? ____________________________________

Why? ______________________________________

How? ______________________________________

Step Four: Personalize the verse: Apply the verse. Glue the promise to a problem.

Step Five: Pray the verse into your life: Ask God to make the verse a reality in your life today.

Colossians 3:1–2

"Since then you have been raised with Christ, set your hearts on things above where Christ is seated at the right hand of God. Set your minds on things above, not on earthly things."

Taking it to Heart:

Day One: Pressing On!

1. Make the scripture memory plan work according to your personal learning style, changing it up to meet your needs.
2. Follow the meditation process throughout your week of memorizing the verse.
3. Review the previous week's verse each day as you learn a new one.
4. Take the index spiral or card with you wherever you go today and review the verse as you travel in your car, brush your teeth, do laundry, wait in line, before you eat each meal, and before going to sleep tonight.

Days 2–6: Living Intentionally!

1. Repeat Day One exercises each day.
2. Look for opportunities to share the verse. Type it out each time you send an email (No copying and pasting!) or try to work it into at least one conversation each day.
3. Give your mind an assignment as you go to bed each night. Try to quote as many memory verses as you can

before falling asleep. In the morning, do not let your feet touch the floor until you attempt to quote your verse for the week.

Day Seven: Review Day

1. Try to write out the passage in your prayer journal without looking at your index spiral. Check to see how you did. Make note of any special insights you discovered or ways you have practically applied the passage to your life.
2. Contact your accountability partner and share your verse and how God used it in your life. Did it help in overcoming temptation? Did the truth of the verse convict you or sharpen your character in any way?

Developing a Heart of Obedience

"The scriptures were given not to increase our knowledge, but to change our lives." D.L. Moody[5]

In order to love the Lord with all our heart, soul, and might (Deut. 6:5), we first gain knowledge of him through memorizing and meditating on his Word. Then Jesus takes our love a step further in John 14:21 when he says, "He who has my commandments and **keeps** them, he it is who loves me ..." Memorizing and meditating is the *heart* and *soul* of Deuteronomy 6:5, while John 14:21 is the *might!* After rehearsing the truth through meditation, we take the stage of real life and live it! (2 Cor. 10:5) As we fall in love with the Lord, we desire to serve him, which takes some of our own muscle. Application takes our strength—that is, realizing that our strength alone will not make us into a godly person, but

5 Cynthia Heald, *Becoming a Woman of Excellence* (Colorado Springs: NavPress 2005) p. 39

our obedience to the power of God's Word. I have spent too much time rationalizing the lies that say such things as, "I am not good enough" or "God could never forgive this." Instead we must "stop *rationalizing* our lies and start *realizing* God's truth" (John 8:32).

Once I had developed the discipline of memorizing and meditating on God's Word, I realized that in order to move forward in my journey of delighting in God, the Word had to seep up from my heart and overflow into the ruts of my life. The ruts are those selfish desires and actions that have become ungodly habits that mark a person's life. I began to ask God weekly to give me opportunities to apply his word in my everyday circumstance. The truth of 1 Corinthians 3:18 became evident in my life, "and we who with unveiled faces all reflect the Lord's glory are being transformed into His likeness with ever increasing glory, which comes from the Lord, who is the Spirit." Transformation begins when we choose to walk in his truth. John 8:32 tells us that the truth (God's Word) will set us free from the ruts of life. He unveils the ruts in our lives and replaces them with his glory. I have learned that obedience will only come when I admit my inability to change on my own. I cannot do anything without him and his Word in me.

I tried God's Word on and realized that I needed to make some alterations in my attitudes, thinking, and actions. He proved himself to be the master tailor of my life. When I put on the Lord Jesus Christ (Romans 13:14), he takes the scissors and needles of his Word and remakes me into a new creation, empowering me to overcome the tests of life. Since the Word is Christ, we clothe ourselves with the truths and promises contained in the Word by first putting it into our minds and hearts and then walking it out.

Mobilize

Mobilize the Word into Your Life

So many times in my life I have been caught in the trap of thinking that if things were going to change in my life then it was up to me, and me alone! I have tried to lose weight, to get along with a difficult person, and even get organized with my own strength. I would be successful for a little while, but eventually I would fall back into my old way of thinking and acting. I needed a way to be constantly reminded of truth that would set me free. In my first year of memorizing scripture, I discovered that I had to live out a scripture in order for it to be cemented in my heart and mind.

The third finger of our grip is the tallest and strongest part of the grip. The third step in the process of getting a handle on God's Word is applying the truths of scripture to our real-life circumstances. This step is mobilizing the Word into your life. To mobilize means to organize resources to be ready for action. Through memorizing and meditating on God's Word, you prepared your mind, just as 1 Peter 1:13 instructs us to prepare our minds for action. James 1:22 exhorts us to not merely listen to the Word—memorizing and meditating on it—but to "do what it says." Second Peter 1:5 presents this process of developing godliness, first through knowledge, and then through applying self-control to what you know. When we do not discipline ourselves for godliness our lives begin to implode. Proverbs 25:28 says, "Like a city whose walls are broken down is a man who lacks self-control." Rebuilding the broken things in our lives takes God's grace and truth mixed with our application of self-control. I call this *proving the Word.*

Proving the Word simply means taking the Word of God and applying it to your real-life circumstances through doing what it says: Living the Word (James 1:22), praying its truth over a person or situation, praying the Word (John 15:7) and breaking the silence of lies through speaking aloud the Word in response to whatever life brings your way, or speaking the Word.

Prove the Word

Geometry was my favorite subject in high school. Most people groan whenever I disclose this fact. However, I think it was more about the teacher than the subject! One of the things I enjoyed was solving proofs. The teacher would write a statement on the chalkboard and then ask us to prove that statement true or false using the truths or theorems that we had been given. In the same way, the Holy Spirit reminds us of everything Jesus has said to us in his Word, empowering us to live out those truths—proving them to be true. God gives us his word and asks us to prove it true.

Proving the Word is another way to say, "live by the Spirit." When I would hear a sermon on living by the Spirit and not by the flesh, I would get all pumped up, but then fall flat on my face by the next day. I didn't have a practical way of living by the spirit. I need practicality. This is wonderfully illustrated in the story of a pilot as told by Neil Anderson in his devotional book, *Daily in Christ.*

THE HOLY SPIRIT'S GUIDANCE

Romans 8:14: "For all who are being led by the Spirit of God, these are sons of God."

A young pilot had just passed the point of no return when the weather changed for the worse. Visibility dropped to a matter of feet as fog descended to the earth. Putting total trust in the cockpit instruments was a new experience to him, for the ink was still wet on the certificate verifying that he was qualified for instrument flying.

The landing worried him the most. His destination was a crowded metropolitan airport he wasn't familiar with. In a few minutes he would be in radio contact with the tower. Until then, he was alone with his thoughts. His instructor had practically forced him to memorize the rule book. He didn't care for it at the time, but now he was thankful.

Finally he heard the voice of the air traffic controller. "I'm going to put you on a holding pattern," the controller radioed. *Great!* thought the pilot. However, he knew that his safe landing was in the hands of this person. He had to draw upon his previous instructions and training, and trust the voice of an air traffic controller he couldn't see. Aware that this was no time for pride, he informed the controller, "This is not a seasoned pro up here. I would appreciate any help you could give me."

> "You've got it!" he heard back.
>
> For the next 45 minutes, the controller gently guided the pilot through the blinding fog. As course and altitude corrections came periodically, the young pilot realized the controller was guiding him around obstacles and away from potential collisions. With the words of the rule book firmly placed in his mind, and with the gentle voice of the controller, he landed safely at last.
>
> The Holy Spirit guides us through the maze of life much like that air traffic controller. The controller assumed that the young pilot understood the instructions of the flight manual. His guidance was based on that. Such is the case with the Holy Spirit: He can guide us if we have a knowledge of God's Word and His will established in our minds.[6]

To remember the scriptures I am memorizing, I realized that the verses would have to be proven to be true in my life. I would have to do what the Word says in order to protect myself from being simply a hearer and "quoter" of the Word. Using the meditation process as my starting point, I began to pray and ask God to use the verse in my everyday circumstances. I asked him to open my eyes to opportunities to apply the memory verses to conversations, challenges, and even to my thought life. Looking closer into the verse, I would ask myself questions such as:

---

6 Neil Anderson, *Daily in Christ* (Eugene, OR: Harvest House Publishers) January1 entry.

- Is there a sin to confess?
- Is there an action to take?
- Is there a command to obey?
- Is there a promise to claim?

I then began to record how God proved his word through specific verses. I even kept a list on my computer entitled, "Scriptures God Has Proved in my Life."

Finally, I looked for opportunities to share these proving experiences with others. As you can see, proving the Word is an intentional act of will. Proving the Word is choosing to think, talk, and walk the way of truth (Ps. 119:30). It is something that happens, not by accident, but with discipline and diligence.

Live the Word

I discovered a verse that revolutionized my attitude, and I hope it will do the same for you. Proverbs 15:15 says, "All the days of the afflicted are bad, but a cheerful heart has a continual feast" (NASB). The week I was memorizing and meditating on this verse I was to fly to California to speak at a workshop. The morning my plane was to depart, I arrived at the airport two hours early due to all the extra security. I checked my bags and went through the security line with ease. It was going to be a great day! Shortly after this thought went through my mind, I was greeted at the gate with the word "cancelled" flashing at the check-in desk. The waiting area sat eerily vacant and my first instinct was to panic and enter into a really bad day. The Holy Spirit tapped me on the shoulder and the words of Proverbs 15:15 swept through my mind. I laughed out loud and then looked around to see if anyone had seen me! God was up to something! He was calling me to try his Word and see if it was true. So I took the challenge and set out to prove his Word. At that moment, I chose to have a cheerful heart and looked to see what feast might await me.

After standing in a long line for about thirty minutes, all the while rehearsing in my mind the truths of Proverbs 15:15, I discovered that all flights to Dallas had been cancelled due to bad weather. My itinerary had called for a stopover in Dallas and then a flight to Oakland. As I stepped up to the counter, I greeted the clerk with a smile, as I had chosen to be cheerful. She said, "I am sorry, but you will have to change airlines, which means you will have to walk to baggage pick-up and then take a tram to another terminal to board your plane."

I replied cheerfully, "Not a problem, I didn't care for my original airline and I need the exercise!"

She continued with her bad news, "You will be on a non-stop flight, arriving in Oakland two hours early."

My dimples deepened as I grinned even bigger and said to myself, "Continual feast!" I entered the airplane and discovered that I had the entire row of seats all to myself. I was able to read, study, and rest for the entire three-hour flight. It was quite a feast! I had tried God's Word, chosen to obey its truth, and found it to be true.

Pray the Word

I had an aha moment as I memorized John 15:7 (NASB): "If you abide in me and my words abide in you, ask whatever you wish, and it will be done for you." The phrase "my words abide in you" took on a whole new meaning as I mediated on the truth. If I am hiding God's Word in my heart, then when I ask the truth of his Word to be true in my life, God answers! So a powerful and sure way to prove the Word in your life is through prayer. As I pray and ask God to apply truth to my life, I also look for opportunities to pray the verse for myself or others. Psalm 107:20 became "Charlene's verse" once I received the heartbreaking news that she had been diagnosed with multiple sclerosis. The verse reminded me of the healing power of God's Word. I began to pray, "Lord, send your Word to Charlene, healing her and delivering her from destruction." I told Charlene that I was praying Psalm 107:20 for her each day. A couple of weeks later we passed one another in the hallway at church. She took hold of my arm and with great excitement said, "Nancy, you inspired me with your memorized scriptures and so now I want to memorize scripture. So whenever you see me, ask me to quote for you the verse I am memorizing." I was so humbled to know that God used me as an instrument of inspiration in Charlene's life; but more amazing was how God was answering my prayer of sending his Word and healing Charlene. The answer did not look like I had anticipated—a miraculous healing. But God was sending his Word into Charlene's life as she hid it in her heart. Now I watch expectantly to see how his healing and deliverance will come!

Speak the Word

As I was waiting for my turn to speak at an event, I listened to three women give their testimonies of how God had been working in their lives. As the first woman gave the details of her story, one of my memory verses came rushing into my mind. I had a divinely given urge to share the scripture with this woman. However, since I was in the audience with hundreds of people, I simply wrote it down so that I could share it with her afterwards. Then the same thing happened with the second woman, and then again with the third woman. The Lord gave me specific scriptures of hope and encouragement for each woman. When the time came for me to walk to the podium to speak, I had to first tell everyone of this wonderful revelation. I stood at that moment and told each woman the verse the Lord had given to me especially for them and their circumstances. That evening after I spoke, all three women came to ask again where their verse was found and to thank me for sharing the truth with them. As I drove home, I praised the Lord for giving me the ability to hide his Word in my heart—not for my sake, but for those who crossed my path that night. I could say with Isaiah, "The Sovereign Lord has given me an instructed tongue, to know the word that sustains the weary. He wakens me morning by morning, wakens my ear to listen like one being taught" (Isa. 50:4).

Jesus instructs his disciples to shout on the housetop whatever he had told them in secret. Matthew 10:24: "There is power in speaking the Words of God." Micah knew that power when he said in Micah 7:7–8, "But as for me, I will watch expectantly for the Lord. I will wait for the God of my salvation. My God will hear me. Do not rejoice over me, O my enemy. Though I fall I will rise; though I dwell in darkness, the Lord is a light for me" (NASB). Micah spoke the truth of who God is aloud to the circumstance. In fact, I memorized Micah's words to proclaim aloud the truth that God is light whenever I find myself in a dark situation. The enemy wants to discourage us when we fail or relapse into sinful habits. Proclaiming aloud this verse gives me hope and power to move out of the darkness of my sin into the forgiving light of God's grace. David also knew the power of crying out to God. He spoke not only his requests for deliverance, but also his proclamations of the truth of God's character. Psalm 57:2: "I will cry to God Most High, to God who accomplishes all things for me" (NASB).

Jesus told his disciples that although he would leave them physically, God was going to send a counselor who would be with them always and would even remind them of everything he had told them when he was with them (John 14:26). When we hide the Word in our hearts, it takes root and remains within our storehouse of truth. When we face a challenge or a temptation, the Holy Spirit will tap us on the shoulder of our heart and speak softly the truth we have hidden there. It is then our part to apply it as healing balm to a wound or as a word of wisdom to a friend. "To speak in the light, what God tells us in the dark and to proclaim aloud what He whispers in our ears" (Matt. 10:27).

This third step of gripping the Word of God is the strongest and perhaps the most character-molding of the grip. Memorizing the Word gives us the knowledge of the Word, while meditation brings that knowledge to light in our own lives, giving us understanding. Then understanding gives us fuel for mobilizing the Word into our lives through living it out, praying it, and speaking it. It moves us from being simply a member of the audience of Christianity to the stage of life where we actively participate in working out the truth of Christianity for his purpose and pleasure (Phil. 2:13). It is what living a life of obedience is all about—experiencing his Word working in us!

James 1:22

"Do not merely listen to the word and so deceive yourselves. Do what it says."

Taking it to Heart:

Day One: Pressing On!

1. Pray, asking God to prove this scripture in your life in a very practical way. Ask him to reveal new insights into this verse.
2. Use the meditation process to cement this verse in your mind.
3. Take the spiral with you wherever you go today and review the verse as you travel in your car, brush your teeth, do laundry, wait in line, before you eat each meal, and before going to sleep tonight.

Days Two–Seven: Living Intentionally!

1. Connect with your accountability partner and share your new verse.
2. Pray the verse for yourself and others.
3. Share the verse with someone each day as an encouragement, in an email, a telephone conversation, or a note.
4. Be alert to opportunities to prove the verse in your life.
5. Find motivation through short-term goals. For example, give the gift of the memorized Word to someone special. Quote your memory verses as a blessing for an individual or for a family member's birthday or special occasion.

Living a Life of Trust

"Those who know your name will trust in you, for you, Lord, have never forsaken those who seek you."
Psalm 9:10

Early one morning, my daughter and I were driving to the state high school baseball championship game. The further we drove, the darker the sky grew as the threat of severe weather surrounded us. Before we knew it, we were in the midst of a dangerous storm with heavy rain, wind, and lightning. Fear gripped both of us as we sought to find shelter from the storm. Piercing my heart and flooding my mind were the words of Psalm 91:1: "He who dwells in the shelter of the Most High, will rest in the shadow of the Almighty." (NASB) I began to shout those words over and over until the rest came to my heart as I was reminded of the Lord with whom I trusted my very life.

As we seek to know the Lord we are commanded to love, we find that our obedience brings about blessing. Through experiencing God in our seeking to know him more intimately and obeying his Word, we discover firsthand the trustworthiness of God. The God who promises is faithful to fulfill those promises (1 Cor. 1:9)! The more we memorize, meditate on, and mobilize God's Word into our lives, the more childlike our faith becomes. We trust him, no matter what the circumstance. As we take in his Word consistently, we begin to take on the responsibilities and rewards of being his chosen ones. Our lives become marked by God's Word and work in our lives.

Mark

Marked by the Word

The Word has marked my life. As Jeremiah was known by others as the man of the Lord of Hosts, I desire to be known by others, not as Nancy, the mother of Sarah and Will or the wife of William or even the Bible study teacher, but as the woman of the Lord of Hosts: A woman of the Word. Hiding God's Word in my heart has given me ownership of his Word. I remember so vividly when I came to the realization that God's Word had become my Word. I was sitting in a church service and as the pastor began to read the text for his sermon, it was as if he was reading my prayer journal. Those were my scriptures; scriptures that I had hidden in my heart and that had been proven true in my life!

After a long week of work, I wearily made the long trek home in the Houston traffic. My eyes were glazed over as I half-heartedly listened to the Christian radio station playing on my car stereo. Then the deejay began interviewing a man who was to be one of the worship leaders that evening at a citywide praise and worship service. My ears perked up as I heard the worship leader say, "I have spent time developing my secret life." That got my attention. I wanted to know more. The deejay asked, "Is it true that you have never completed a college degree, but have been a worship leader for nineteen years?" The worship leader answered, "I have never had to promote myself. The scripture tells us that what is done in secret will be revealed. So I have just worked on my secret life. I started by getting alone in my room as a teenager to sing and play the guitar to the Lord. Then I would sing to the Lord or take a walk and pray. This became a habit and my secret life was revealed as I publicly led others in worship." By this time, I was looking for something to write on as I drove down the freeway. Wow! That is how you live a marked life. This is what has happened to me! I set out to memorize God's Word to renew my mind and increase my ammunition against the enemy, but something greater occurred. The secret times I spent hiding scripture in my heart became evident to those who my life touched.

Gripping God's Word through memorizing, meditating, and mobilizing it in your life will make a profound mark on your life. I have found that God's treasured Word has marked my life spiritually, relationally, and publicly. When the Word has been implanted within your mind and heart, it acts as a gardener. The Word is sharp, so it is a hoe that breaks up the hard places of our hearts, making them more accessible to the seeds of faith God wants to sow in us. When the Word breaks up our hearts, we are more aware of the sin that tries to take root. I find I keep shorter accounts with God, in that my heart is more fertile, allowing conviction to come easier—and God's Word is Miracle-Gro for the heart! God's Word has marked my life spiritually.

After making a commitment to faithfully memorize at least one scripture verse a week, I have been blessed and changed through God's powerful Word. One of the blessings has been that the Word naturally flows out of my mouth during prayer, while leading a Bible study class, while speaking to someone over the phone, or in the midst of a witnessing opportunity.

Relating with others who are grieving, who need advice, or who are just in need of a little encouragement comes with ease now that the Word is stored up in my mind. I used to try to give words of comfort or encouragement, but they seemed empty and without much power. Now sharing the Word comes naturally when relating with others and I see how much power God's Word has to give hope, help, and healing.

When God's Word is stored up in your heart, the Holy Spirit will remind you of the Word with timely precision. Once I discovered 1 Peter 4:11: "If one speaks he should do it as one speaking the very words of God." I realized that hiding God's Word in my heart had equipped me to be a speaker and teacher who would literally speak the very words of God. One Saturday evening, I was soaking in the bathtub, preparing to pamper myself with a pedicure and manicure, when I got a call from my Sunday morning Bible study teacher. She was stranded in an airport due to bad weather and asked if I would be able to teach her class the next day. I laughed out loud and asked if she were serious! You see, our class had about 400 in attendance each week and the thought of me standing before such a large class with a hastily prepared lesson made my heart race. Needless to say, I was a bit surprised and totally unprepared to teach a lesson, or so I thought. After the initial shock, I asked what verse she was planning to teach. She had been teaching through the book of 1 Peter and to my amazement, the verse she gave me to teach a lesson on just happened to be one I had hidden in my heart. I agreed to teach and since it was so late, I prayed, asking the Lord to give me a lesson in the morning. I then went to bed. The Lord woke me up with an outline based on the scripture and reminded me of other memory verses that supported each point. I had an outline and a handout by class time that morning. The verse was 1 Peter 2:9: "But you are a chosen people, a royal priesthood, a holy nation, a people belonging to God, that you may declare the praises of Him who called you out of darkness into His wonderful light." That scripture had marked my life many years before, preparing me for the day I would be called on to teach a lesson of how God marks our lives as chosen, royal, and belonging to Him. I shall never forget that day and how he chose (marked) me to declare his praises!

In Waylon Moore's book *Living God's Word,* Moore tells how the life of Miss Jones, a missionary to China, was dramatically impacted by a verse of scripture which had been given to her by her friend, Dawson Trotman.

Dawson Trotman escorted Miss Jones to the ship that would take her back to the mission field. He prayed for her and shared a scripture with her. Shortly after arriving in China, a civil war broke out and the communists took over the government. This in turn brought about great persecution of all Christians, especially missionaries. Many were killed and some even took their own lives in the face of such great suffering. Miss Jones, however, made it out of China and back to the United States, where she went immediately to visit Mr. Trotman. Upon arriving in his office she explained all that she had witnessed and experienced at the hands of the communists and wanted to thank him for sharing with her the verse of scripture before she departed. She told Mr. Trotman, "I memorized it while traveling across the Pacific. God used it powerfully, shielding me from suicide. Thank you. That verse saved my life."[7]

I want to be a "Dawson Trotman" to someone in my life. Can you imagine the blessing of hearing someone say to you: "Thank you for sharing that Scripture with me, it saved my ... marriage, my relationship with my children, or even ... my life." This can be said to anyone who chooses to allow God's Word to make its mark on his or her life.

I do not ever want to forget how God's Word has marked my life. This is why I write these things down in my journal so that I shall never forget. I have a journal in which I write down my quiet time insights, prayers, sermon notes, Bible study notes, and notes on how God's Word is working in my life. It is a history of my relationship with God and others and a reminder of the marks God's Word has made on my life.

---

7 Waylon B. Moore, *Living God's Word* (Nashville: LifeWay Press, 1997) p.50.

Mark 4:22:

"For nothing is hidden except to be revealed; nor has anything been secret but that it should come to light." (NASB)

Taking it to Heart:

Day One: Pressing On!

1. Pray, asking God to prove this scripture in your life in a very practical way. Ask him to reveal new insights into this verse.
2. Use the meditation process to cement this verse in your mind.
3. Take the spiral with you wherever you go today and review the verse as you travel in your car, brush your teeth, do laundry, wait in line, before you eat each meal, and before going to sleep tonight.
4. Begin making a list of how specific scripture verses have marked your life.
5. Review verses from the past weeks.

Days Two–Seven: Living Intentionally!

6. Connect with your accountability partner and share your new verse.
7. Pray the verse for yourself and others.
8. Share the verse with someone each day as an encouragement, in an email, a telephone conversation, or a note.
9. Be alert to opportunities to prove the verse in your life.

10. Challenge yourself and see if you can talk to yourself or someone else for at least five minutes about the verse you are memorizing this week. Talk about its meaning, ways to apply it to your life, and any other insights you may have gotten from meditating on it.

Momentum

Maintaining Spiritual Momentum

Eating one potato chip has never been easy for me! If I dare open a bag of potato chips, the bottom of the bag becomes my destined finish line. I cannot just eat one chip, and I have learned that I cannot stop eating God's Word. Once I tasted the Word and found such rich flavor, I cannot stop eating it (1 Peter 2:3). People ask me often how I have continued to memorize scripture over the years and the answer is, "I started and I can't quit." This is the last step in getting a grip on God's Word, and it may well be the key to developing a lifestyle of scripture memory. It is not just maintenance or maintaining the status quo, but it is about maintaining and increasing momentum in your journey. These are the things that I do that help me stay on this journey:

Review often what God has done: I began prayer journaling over twenty years ago and since memorizing scripture, I have begun to keep a record of what God has done in my heart and life through his memorized Word. Hebrews 2:1: "For this very reason we must pay closer attention to what we have heard lest we drift away from it." Therefore, keep a journal that you write in often, recording what God has shown you through his Word and how he has proved his Word in your life. Recently I have been taking the time to read over my last completed journal, and using a marker, I highlight the times God has spoken or moved in my life clearly through those scriptures hidden in my heart. So go back occasionally and read through your journal as a reminder of what he has done in your life and as a safeguard to keep you from drifting away from it.

Intentionally pursue a disciplined life: I no longer have to make a daily decision if I am going to memorize scripture. It is a done deal. I intentionally make it a part of my daily routine. First Timothy 6:11: "But you, man of God, flee from all of this and pursue righteousness, godliness, faith, love, endurance and gentleness." We do only those things that we intend on doing! Go after a life of hiding God's Word in your heart. It is an act of the will not necessarily done out of emotion. You just do it!

Develop spiritual fervor: A few years ago, I began to write out in my prayer journal daily this prayer: "Lord, give me a passion for your Word, your ways, your ministry, and your will." It is amazing how God answers such prayers! Romans 12:11: "Never be lacking in zeal, but keep your spiritual fervor, serving the Lord." Fervor is passion and enthusiasm sparked by purpose. Spiritual fervor and a passion to hide God's Word in my heart developed as I followed these principles:

Commit to show up daily to spend time with the Lord: Being faithfully committed to anything is rare in our culture. It is so rare that those who faithfully show up are rewarded greatly. Such was the case with baseball great Cal Ripken when he received the longest standing ovation in a baseball stadium and a new car just for playing in the most consecutive professional baseball games in history. However, when you show up day after day to spend time with the Lord, you can be assured of receiving a crown that will never fade away (1 Peter 5:4). A godly man who influenced my walk with Christ once said, "Nancy, keep standing at the shore and the tide will surely come in." We all go through dry times in our relationship with Christ and it is in those times that we must develop the discipline of standing at the shore, even when we don't see the tide coming. It is a long-term investment that may not show a lot of profit at first, but over time you will reap a harvest of righteousness and peace.

Do the right thing; and when you slip up, try to do the next right thing! They say that if the horse bucks you off, it is best to get back on it! When your well-intended plans do not work out, go back to the drawing board and see where your plan failed. Pick up where you left off, doing the next right thing. "You were running a good race. Who cut in on you and kept your from obeying the truth?" (Gal. 5:7)

Avoid these "Word-chokers" (Mark 4:19): The Lord warned us that if we are not on our guard, worries, deceitfulness of wealth, and desires for other things will choke out the truth of his Word.

Worries of this life: The worries of this life can overwhelm us and before we know it, we are dried out spiritually. When my children were teenagers, there was always a fire to put out. I was often called in to help with a project the night before it was due, give counsel concerning a friend's hurt feelings, or coordinate the snacks for the basketball season. I have learned over the years that I must carve out the time to *refill* my mind with the Word daily before tackling the worries of this life. All these worries in life can begin to choke out the good God is doing with his Word in our hearts. The word becomes watered down. Instead choose to think on the true, noble, right, lovely, admirable, excellent, and praiseworthy things, and then the Word will once again be full strength in your life (Phil. 4:8)!

Deceitfulness of wealth: Our lives can become so overwhelmed by the pursuit of more money, more education, more friends, and more status that our storehouse of heavenly things sits in the shadow of our storehouse of earthly things. Recently we moved from a 2400-square foot home with a two-car garage to a 1300-square foot, two-bedroom condominium with no garage. We began to realize how attached to "things" we had become. What once appeared to us as boxes of wealth have become boxes of junk! I looked at each box and thought to myself, "How deceived I was to fill up that box with things for which I now have no room or time!" You see, when we store up earthly treasures to excess, it only crowds out heavenly treasures, which are timeless and endless treasures given by God for our good and for his pleasure.

Desires for "other things": Saying no to good things is hard for me. As a child of an alcoholic, I learned to be a people-pleaser in order to survive in a chaotic home. I didn't want to rock the boat or be the cause that set my father off in any way. Because of my background, I find that I take on too many "other things" in my life that tend to crowd out the "best things." Titus 2:11–12 is a scripture hidden in my heart which instructs me to say no to "ungodliness and worldly desires and to live sensibly, righteously, and godly in the present age." NASB Now I test these other things that want to choke out truth by asking myself, "Is the thing sensible, righteous and godly?" If it is, then I say "yes," and if it is not, I say "no!"

Begin again each time I falter: When I give in to the Word-chokers and allow them make my life fruitless, I become miserable. I have learned that until the pain of staying the same becomes greater than the pain of change, I will remain fruitless. But when that fruitless pain becomes great, I give way to change and begin again on the journey. These are the steps I take to begin again:

Repent and return *to God*: "Repent then and turn to God, so that your sins may be wiped out, that times of refreshing may come from the Lord" (Acts 3:19). For a fresh start, admit to God and yourself that you have become lax or have failed to keep your commitment. Ask for forgiveness and a fresh start. Whenever we get honest with God and share our heart's desire with him, he is faithful to forgive. He is much like that special friend who no matter how often or seldom you see them, you just take up where you left off, as if no time had passed. Hebrews 12:15 is a truth that set me free from this all-or-nothing thinking. It says, "See to it that no one misses the grace of God …" When I first memorized that verse, I focused on giving grace to others when they hurt me or made mistakes. I have finally realized that I am a part of that "no one." I am learning to accept God's grace that says, "Nancy, you didn't hide my Word in your heart this week, but that is okay, and just begin *again* today." I extend myself grace when I do not keep up with the commitment of a weekly verse. I figure that God wants me to spend an extra week or two on some verses or that I need an extra week to just review the verses I already stored in my heart.

Get up! Don't allow the enemy to fill your mind with lies such as "I can't" and "give up!" Instead, listen to this truth: "Do not gloat over me, my enemy. Though I have fallen, I will rise. Though I sit in darkness the Lord will be my light." (Mic. 7:8). Tell the enemy that you may have fallen down in your commitment, but that by the grace of God you are getting back up!

Don't look back! Don't dwell on unmet goals or feelings of failure. Instead set your sights on the path, taking the next step forward (Phil. 3:12–16). Start where you are and ask God for a new verse and to do something new in your life (Isa. 43:18–19).

Keep Going: Recently I pulled into a one-way entrance to our church parking lot. As I drove through the narrow entrance, I realized that a huge truck blocked me in. It was parked at an angle, blocking me from entering the parking lot. I could not go backwards because it led back into the path of the freeway access road. I was stuck! I had about three minutes to get to a meeting, so I called several people that I knew were inside the church building to seek help. Finally, the driver of the truck appeared and moved his truck, freeing me to move forward and park. That was a great reminder to me of how we do allow those "chokers" in our lives to be roadblocks to our spiritual growth. It also showed me that all I needed to do was call for help and eventually it came—giving me power to move ahead.

Once you are back on the road to growth, keep moving forward. You never stand still spiritually. You are either going forward or backward! "Let us not grow weary in doing good, for at the proper time you will reap a harvest if you do not give up" (Gal. 6:9). So get up and keep going in your pursuit of God's truth.

Follow God's prompting to pass it on: When you become passionate about something, you can't help but share it with those around you. The power of God's Word in your life can be multiplied when you are obedient to share with others these words of life, hope, and help. Success in your life breeds success in others. Each time I am asked to teach an individual or present a seminar to a group about how to get a grip on God's Word, I can't start talking quickly enough! After a few years of teaching people how to memorize scripture, I was constantly being asked, "Nancy, do you have a book that explains further what you have just taught?" This book is the result of a God-given desire to share with others this incredible habit that will transform a life.

During the first year of my personal scripture memory journey, when I committed to the Lord to memorize one scripture verse a week for fifty-two weeks, I learned to persevere through challenges. My goal was to be able to quote all fifty-two verses at the end of the year. My goal was my motivation. My goal was the vision that I kept before me each week as I began learning a new verse. Bill Parcels, the former head coach of the Dallas Cowboys, once said, "This year will bring many challenges, but it will not lessen the vision." That was my mindset as I journeyed that first year of scripture memorization. That is the key to consistency in disciplining your life for godliness or for physical health. All-or-nothing thinking is common among today's dieter. We begin a diet plan and at the first hint of trouble we quit, telling ourselves that we will begin next week. Unfortunately, one week becomes one month, and before we know it we are desperately in a never-ending yo-yo cycle of weight loss and weight gain, never reaching that goal we had envisioned. We turn in to "should've, could've, and would've" people, always making excuses and living in regret. The same is true in our spiritual discipline, and the enemy is having a celebration at our expense, for he is keeping us from enjoying all that we have as children of the King.

As you begin this journey of scripture memorization, remember that each part of gripping the Word builds a tighter grasp on it. Starting with the "pinky" finger of the grip, you will memorize the Word with godly purpose, manned with a plan that guards against legalism and furnishes a firm foundation for which to follow through with the commitment. Meditating on God's Word takes time, but yields the accomplishment of a deeper knowledge of scripture. This knowledge leads to the heart of the grip, mobilizing the Word through application, or proving the Word. When you mobilize scripture in your life, you find that God marks your life in dramatic ways—just as a wedding band on your left ring finger marks you as one committed to another in marriage. The Word will mark your life spiritually, relationally, and publicly. The thumb of a fist holds all the fingers of the grip together, just as practicing spiritual momentum will allow you to grip tightly God's Word for a lifetime.

- **Memorize the Word with purpose and manned with a plan.**
- **Meditate: Chew on the Word and ponder its meaning.**
- **Mobilize the Word into your life.**
- **Mark: Marked by the Word.**
- **Momentum: Maintaining spiritual momentum.**

God's Word, once rooted in your heart, will bring you joy beyond measure because it gives you knowledge of your creator; a willing, obedient heart; and a deeper trust in the one who loves you like no other.

Romans 12:11:

"Never be lacking in zeal, but keep your spiritual fervor, serving the Lord.

Taking it to Heart

Day One: Pressing On!

1. Keep a list of scriptures to memorize

- Choose a *variety* of topics and authors to stay balanced in your knowledge.
- Choose verses and passages *that relate to you* and your current life circumstances.
- Some *suggested verses* and passages:
    - Philippians 2 (humility)
    - Psalm 100 (praise)
    - Isaiah 55 (the Word)
    - 2 Corinthians 4 (ministry)
    - A Year's Supply of Memory Verses (see appendix)

Day Two and Forward: Living Intentionally!

1. Develop a plan for review that works for you!
2. Avoid Word-chokers—list those that are most tempting to you and ask God's help in pursuing a godly lifestyle.
3. Begin again each time you fall:
    - Repent

- Get up
- Don't look back
- Keep going

A Year's Supply of Memory Verses

Scripture Memorization

1. Jeremiah 15:16
2. Psalm 1:2–3
3. Psalm 119:30
4. Deuteronomy 30:14
5. Hebrews 2:1
6. Colossians 3:16
7. Matthew 6:19–21

Overcoming Temptation

1. Psalm 119:11
2. 1 Corinthians 10:13
3. Titus 2:11–12
4. 2 Corinthians 12:9
5. Micah 7:7–8
6. Psalm 27:13–14
7. 2 Corinthians 10:4
8. Psalm 18:28–29

Renewing and Preparing the Mind

1. Romans 12:2
2. Colossians 3:1–2
3. Psalm 51:12
4. 1 Peter 1:13
5. 2 Corinthians 4:16
6. Psalm 94:19
7. 2 Corinthians 10:5

Receiving Direction and Guidance

1. Micah 6:8
2. Psalm 90:12
3. Psalm 143:8
4. John 14:26
5. John 16:33
6. Isaiah 55:11
7. Psalm 119:105

Developing Godly Character

1. 2 Peter 1:4
2. 2 Corinthians 4:7
3. Luke 6:45
4. Philippians 2:12–13
5. Hebrews 12:11
6. 2 Corinthians 1:20
7. Proverbs 15:15

Establishing Prayer Life

1. John 15:7
2. Matthew 21:22
3. Psalm 57:2
4. Psalm 37:4
5. 1 Peter 4:7
6. Colossians 1:9–10
7. Ephesians 3:20

Sharing with Others

1. Zephaniah 3:17
2. Psalm 3:3

3. Isaiah 50:4
4. Matthew 11:28–30
5. Romans 5:8
6. Romans 3:22–24
7. Romans 6:23
8. Ephesians 2:8-9
9. Ephesians 2:10